Friends Are Where
You Find Them

May the friendship we
share never cease to
end.
   And may each birthday
be happier than the
one before.
     Happy Birthday Jo
   Mary Ann
        Mike
          &
        Michael
       (The Merrisses)

Friends
Are Where You
Find Them

*Personal Experiences That Convey
The Universal Meaning of "Friend"*

*Selected by Tina Hacker
Illustrated by Carl Cassler*

HALLMARK EDITIONS

Friends Are Where You Find Them

The Adventure of Friendship

Learning to accept people for what they are — themselves — is a key to lasting friendships. Grove Patterson suggests that there are many such friendships in the world waiting to be found.

Hazlitt, the 19th-century British essayist, wrote: "One cannot expect people to be other than they are." That idea has guided me on the greatest adventure of my life — the adventure of friendship....

For to be a friend you have to care about people, what they think, what they feel, what they suffer. If you just don't like people, you may still be cordial to acquaintances, but friendship is no go. You must try to understand people, their hopes and fears and aspirations....

Friendship, to me, is an intangible thing, a kind of circle which completely surrounds another person, taking him in with all his good points and all his bad, enveloping him in his entirety. If I come to like a man and a friendship is formed, it is because I have discerned something likeable and lovable deep within him, something of character and fineness, although from time to time he may, as we all do, violate that which is fine and which is customarily a part of him. If he is my friend, there are two things which I shall not think of doing: first, I shall not hurt him, and second, I shall not cross him off my list because he was drunk or disorderly or thoughtless. To me it is cruel to criticize a friend in other than a light way. I prefer to leave criticism to his mere acquaintances. Inasmuch as they are not his friends they cannot hurt him....

I am sure there are more good friends and good friendships in the world than we realize. From close observation of human beings I have come to the conclusion that the average person is better, not worse, than he seems to be. I have more than once discovered that men whom their fellows call selfish, ungenerous, hard, are almost daily engaged in the odds and ends of a thousand little kind and thoughtful acts.

I have found many a soft conscience in a hard coat and many of the deeper qualities of friendship in an inarticulate man.

One who is genuinely friendly ought not to be too critical of his acquaintances who are tactless, undiplomatic, and rarely express thanks or show gratitude. So many feel deeply, but do not have the gift of expression. Some who seem rude are only shy. Some who seem ungrateful are only timid. On the other side, there are people who find it easier to talk than feel. These unfortunates lack the master quality of sincerity. Insincerity may have a pleasant sound but rings no silver bells of truth. Insincerity is the tinkling cymbal of human relationship....

There is no more enduring thing in life than real friendship. If it is not enduring, then it is not real, and has never quite found its way from the far-flung fields of acquaintance to the inner circle of devotion.

Something Belong Friendship

True friends are never forgotten. In John Reddy's story an American airman returns to a South Pacific island to build a school for the natives who saved his life and befriended him during World War II.

In June 1963 (Lt.) Hargesheimer and his 17-year-old son, Dick, arrived in Rabaul. They loaded 400 sacks of cement and other materials on an ancient motor vessel and set out for Nantambu.

Word of their coming had preceded them, and hundreds of natives were on hand to greet them. Early next morning, the whole group set to work to clear the three-acre site near the village of Ewasse....

The formal dedication took place July 11, 1964, and once more Hargesheimer flew to New Britain for the occasion....Speaking in pidgin, Hargesheimer explained that the school was a gift from the American people, not from his government, and that the money came in small amounts from ordinary individuals who were grateful to the men, women and children of New Britain for their help to American airmen in the war. He said he realized that the school was being officially named the Airmen's Memorial School, but he felt that the natives described the school best in their own words. Those words, he said, are: "Something belong friendship."

The Art of Paying a Compliment

It takes time and patience to learn how to pay a compliment, writes J. Donald Adams, but the rewards are well worth the effort.

One of the best ways to smooth relations with other people is to be adept at the art of paying a compliment. The sincere, appreciative remark helps the other fellow to realize his own inherent worth. And, what is more, the ability to pay a compliment bolsters our own ego — which is not a bad thing either.

We never forget a compliment that has deeply pleased us, nor do we forget the person who made it. Yet often the luster of praise is needlessly dimmed by awkwardness in the manner of its giving. Like all ventures in human relations, the art of paying a compliment takes thought and practice. We have all experienced the remorse of having our praise fall flat because we chose the wrong time to give it or the wrong language to couch it in.

According to Leonard Lyons, a compliment of the right sort was paid Toscanini by Judith Anderson when she saw him after a concert.

"She didn't say I had conducted well," said the maestro. "I knew that. She said I looked handsome." It is human nature to enjoy praise for something we are not noted for. When someone calls attention to an unadvertised facet of our personality it makes him forever our friend.

Chin Lip Is My Man

A Chinese-Siamese teaches author Louis S. Leavitt that in true friendship, the one who profits most serves best.

The man who taught me most? His name is Chin Lip.

When I first saw him, he was standing with his thick legs spread wide, his hamlike hands hanging loosely. His cotton home-dyed jacket failed to meet by six inches across his broad chest; his knee-length, once-white trousers were held up by a wide silver-ornamented belt. A battered felt hat topped his close-clipped black hair.

This half-caste Chinese-Siamese was plainly angry. His black eyes snapped. Not understanding Siamese, I could but watch as words erupted from his wide mouth full of teeth blackened by years of betel chewing, and a thin trickle of betel-red saliva drooled from each corner of his mouth.

I had, through an interpreter, simply asked to employ him, his bullock, and his high, two-wheeled cart to haul cement from a boat landing several miles downriver to my camp where a hydroelectric power plant was to be built. But his answer was clearly a "No!"…I was stumped. If Chin Lip held fast in his refusal to use his cart and bull under my employment, every bull-cart owner in the Pong valley would do likewise. And 200 barrels of cement and hundreds of pieces of heavy pipe were at the river landing! Chin Lip was the key pin — he had to be won over. How this was accomplished is immaterial to this yarn. Chin Lip and I became good friends.

A year sped by. The power plant was built and in operation. But Chin Lip would not enter it. He was afraid of no living man, but he had a mighty respect for the dead and that power plant. The struggle to gain his confidence started all over again, but there came the day when in childlike trust he placed one of his big, grimy paws into my hand and we walked in together.

Every day we repeated the performance until at last he walked in alone and I persuaded him to take hold of the controls and start and stop the water wheel. I can still see his face beaming as he saw the machinery take on life. It was a great day for him and for me, to see fear overcome and faith born.

Then came another day when I lay helpless in bed, in pain. The only food I was able to retain was orange juice, and there were no oranges on that side of Siam! Chin Lip stood looking down on me. I was too weak to talk to him. Three days later he returned and stood in my door as the sun sank behind the jungle-clad hills. Held out before him was a basket filled with oranges. His robust figure was slumped with fatigue, but his face was shining. Here were the oranges my cook had told him I needed to restore me to health. Chin Lip had walked 75 hard miles over a high mountain range to the east coast of the Siamese peninsula, had gathered up all the oranges that remained at the tag end of the season, and had returned — a 150-mile hike in three days!

Another year rolled by — and I was going home. As we floated down the river in a dugout, Chin Lip held the paddle, and when we boarded the little coastal steamer that was to carry me the first lap of my journey, Chin Lip climbed the rope ladder behind me. He had never been on a steamship before, but he was not afraid. If it was safe for me, it was safe for him.

We stood by the rail saying good-by. Off came his hat, and out of it he took two colored prints. They were his treasures, but he wanted me to have them. I grasped one of his dirty hands in

both of mine and gave it a squeeze as he swung a leg over the rail and climbed down....

Yes, Chin Lip taught me the most. From him I learned consideration for other men, regardless of race or creed. From him I learned that a man is only as good as his principles; and that righteousness is not a virtue peculiar to any one race alone. From him I learned the power of faith, the endurance of hope, the blessedness of charity, the omnipresence of love. From him I learned that gratitude is a precious jewel to be brought out where men can see it. From Chin Lip I learned that "He Profits Most Who Serves Best."

New Windows on the World

Louise Levitas learns a valuable lesson in friendship from a talented photographer who is equally talented in making friends wherever he goes.

Some people believe that friends are found by luck or accident; that if you do not run into kind, warmhearted folks on your journey through life, then you will not have lots of friends.

This is the reason such people give for being lonely — but the truth is just the opposite. Every man's friends are a reflection of himself, of the interest he takes in the rest of the world. It was Pat Semple who taught me this secret.

Pat was a good photographer. His talent for making friends, for capturing the essence of a personality in a flash, was what made his pictures so good. His wife, Mavis, sometimes complained about his "social itch" (her name for it). She didn't have the time or the interest to gad about, she said. Housekeeping and the children kept her too busy. But Pat!

"We start out for a walk to the movies, and I find he's saying hello to people I never saw before! Why, he knows everyone on this block," she said, "and I don't even know the family in the next apartment! I can't imagine how he does it."

One day, at the shoemaker's, I found out.

The shop was a hole in the wall; the bent, wizened old man seemed scarcely aware of the world outside his door. But when Pat came in his face livened up. He jumped from his chair to greet Mavis' husband, and I listened to their conversation in astonishment. They discussed neither leather nor shoes, but the school marks of the shoemaker's grandson and Pat's two boys.

"We're old friends," Pat explained after we left the shop. "First time I stepped in there, I found out Nick came from Greece when he was a young man, and we started talking about the ancient Greeks — Plato, Aristotle, Socrates. It developed that Nick was quite a philosopher himself."

This work-stained old cobbler — a philosopher? I'd been buying his services for years, seeing only the shoes in his hands. But Pat had looked into the old man's face the first day — and discovered a wonderful human being.

The people who might be our friends are all around us — neighbors, storekeepers, co-workers; those we meet at parties, on business trips, or sitting next to us in church. But, like Pat, we have to open our eyes and recognize them.

Happiness to Share

Major S. P. Matzner finds out that an act of friendship can chase away loneliness no matter how far from home you might be.

When I came to Sydney...I didn't know anyone in Australia. The second night after my arrival I was strolling along George Street, window-shopping, watching people coming from the movies. Perhaps loneliness could be read in my face.

A young man and his girl were coming from the opposite direction, laughing and chatting with each other. The girl looked at me, stopped, came over to me and said, "Please, smile for us."

I smiled. She said, "That's better. Thank you," and walked on, arm in arm with her young man. I never saw her again and I don't know why she wanted me to share her happiness. But I went away smiling and I've never felt lonely in Australia since.

The Mirror of Friendship

Friendship brings out the best in people, even rising above language barriers, as related in this personal experience by Elizabeth Mauske.

On her frequent trips on foot to Temuco, an old Araucanian Indian woman used always to bring my mother a few partridge eggs or a handful of berries. My mother spoke no Araucanian beyond the greeting *"Mai-mai,"* and the old woman knew no Spanish, but she drank tea and ate cake with many an appreciative giggle. We girls stared fascinated at her layers of colorful hand-woven clothing, her copper bracelets and coin necklaces, and we vied with each other in trying to memorize the singsong phrase she always spoke on rising to leave.

At last we learned the words by heart and repeated them to the missionary, who translated them for us. They have stayed in my mind as the nicest compliment ever uttered:

"I shall come again, for *I like myself* when I'm near you."

My Friend, Mr. Dickens

When she was just a little girl, Kate Douglas Wiggin met her literary idol — the great English novelist Charles Dickens. In this selection she recalls how she boldly approached the author. Between them a warm friendship developed which neither one would ever forget.

I never knew how it happened; I had no plan, no preparation, no intention, certainly no provocation; but invisible ropes pulled me out of my seat, and speeding up the aisle, I planted myself breathlessly and timorously down, an unbidden guest, in the seat of honor. I had a moment to recover my equanimity, for Dickens was looking out the window, but he turned suddenly and said with justifiable surprise:

"God bless my soul, child, where did you come from?"

My heart was in my mouth, but there was still room to exercise my tongue, which was generally the case. I was frightened, but not so completely frightened as if I had been meeting a stranger. You see I knew him, even if he did not know me; so I became immediately autobiographical, although palpitating with nervousness. I had to tell him, I thought, where I came from, who I was, where I was going, or how could I account for myself and my presence beside him in Mr. Osgood's seat? So I began, stammeringly, to answer his question:

"I came from Hollis, Maine, and I'm going to Charlestown to visit my uncle. My mother and her cousin went to your reading last night, but of course three couldn't go from the same family, it was so expensive, so I stayed at home. Nora, that's my little sister, is left behind in Hollis. She's too small to go on a journey, but she wanted to go to the reading dreadfully. There was a lady there who had never heard of Betsey Trotwood, and had only read two of your books!"

"Well, upon my word!" he said. "You do not mean to say that *you* have read them!"

"Of course!" I replied; "every one of them but

the two that we are going to buy in Boston, and some of them six times….I do skip some of the very dull parts once in a while; not the short dull parts, but the long ones."

He laughed heartily. "Now, that is something that I hear very little about," he said. "I distinctly want to learn more about those very long dull parts."

…It was not long before one of my hands was in his, and his arm around my waist, while we talked of many things. They say, I believe, that his hands were "undistinguished" in shape, and that he wore too many rings. Well, those criticisms must come from persons who never felt the warmth of his handclasp! For my part, I am glad that Pullman chair cars had not come into fashion, else I should never have experienced the joy of snuggling up to Genius, and of being distinctly encouraged in the attitude.

Friends Anonymous

Victoria W. Ferguson and her family live on a little farm outside New York City. There they discover that strangers befriended make friends ...if only anonymously.

Ours is the yellow cabin with the red door on a busy highway about 30 miles from New York City. Sooner or later you may run out of gas within sight of us. We know the number of the nearest garage; help yourself to the phone and have a drink of spring water.

When we bought our small farm, we wanted to move to it at once. The house was already occupied, and the only thing available was the empty fruit-and-vegetable stand conveniently located for customers but not such a choice location for a residence. Yet we converted it into a home.

Friends said, "But will you like the traffic?" Or "Don't people annoy you asking to use the phone, borrow the jack, water for the car, a drink for the baby?"

But the truth is, it isn't what other people do that matters, but how you react to them. And since we choose to live by the highway, we choose to like people.

Years ago, when I thanked my father for a special favor, he vouchsafed a tip with a magnet attached: "When you want someone to like you, ask him to do you a kindness." This is the first cousin to the familiar, "Where your treasure is there your heart will be also."

When these strangers from the highway ask some small favor of me, if I grant it *cheerfully*, and thereby contribute to their well-being, that contribution is part of myself. A little of my heart has gone out to them, I invest in them, in them lies a little of my treasure....

Last New Year's Eve, a snowstorm blew up. We decided to cancel our date and stay home so we wouldn't see the New Year in shoveling out. We sat at a table and played some family games we hadn't played since the boys were little. It was nearing midnight and we were going to sing *Auld Lang Syne* and drink a sleep-inducing hot chocolate.

Suddenly we heard a car too near the house for comfort. It had skidded dangerously and was stuck in a snowdrift a few feet from our kitchen window. We had stayed at home to avoid shoveling, but as the year ended we were helping dig a stranger out of our snowbank, "taking a cup of kindness yet," not for Auld Lang Syne but to help a stranger. For a stranger befriended is sure to become a friend, even if only anonymous.

You're Welcome

On a tour of the United States, Barbara Wace not only discovers the vast beauty of America — she discovers the warmth and friendliness of the American people.

I had merely asked the way by bus, but the elderly couple in the jalopy insisted on driving me to the tree-shaded street where I was staying. "Why should you bother to go so far out of your way?" I asked. The man, face tanned to leather by the blazing Kansas sun, smiled as he answered: "It's nice to be nice to people. That's why."

After a 10,000-mile bus trip through 28 states and three Canadian provinces, this is the sort of memory I have brought back with me. It was just such people as these who taught me, an English girl, that the warmth and kindliness of Americans have nothing to do with dollars and cents. They spring from the heart.

Last summer I bought a bus ticket from Washington, D. C., to San Francisco and back, routed to look up various friends who had visited us in England during the war. I was to stop at Crossville in Tennessee; at Louisville, Denver, San Francisco, Vancouver, Milwaukee, and at Hancock in New Hampshire. But there were still great spaces on the map, spaces I then believed to be friendless miles.

Now I know better....

My mother wrote from England. "When you have seen that marvelous country and all those kind, warm people, you will have something you will never lose — memories you can cherish, whatever happens afterward." And then, referring to our GI wartime guests, "Remember how they used to say: 'You're welcome.' That's what it will be like, I know."

Mother must have guessed there'd be people like "Aunt Bessie." Since that September evening Hillsboro, where Aunt Bessie lives, is no longer just a little town in the vast expanse of Oregon. It's a place with a welcome.

As I sipped a Coca-Cola at a roadside cafe where the bus had stopped for a ten-minute break, I saw an advertisement for the Hillsboro County Fair. I had always wanted to see a county fair, to compare it with its English counterpart.

On the spur of the moment I arranged with the driver for a stopover.

The sun was setting as I approached the small hotel. "Sorry, full up," said the desk clerk. "It's the fair, you know. There's nowhere else in town."

The chemist's shop in England is always the place where you can find local information. Perhaps the drugstore, I thought, will be the same. Dragging my typewriter and heavy suitcase three blocks down the street, I found Doc behind the prescription counter, and three women customers. All entered into my problem, but nobody, it seemed, took lodgers.

"Mother would love to put you up," suddenly said a voice from the end of the store, where a young man was standing in the shadow. "I know what it's like not to have any place to stay. I was in the Pacific."

Desperate, I suggested that he call her. When he came smiling back, he said: "Mother says she'll have supper ready by the time we get there."

Next evening, when I had boarded my north-bound Greyhound again — after a day at the fair with the whole family, including daughter Leila and her five children — I waved good-bye to Aunt Bessie and Jack, and turned to put my hatbox on the rack. It felt heavier. Inside was a neatly packed parcel. And there was a note.

"Come back soon," it said, "and let us show you more of Oregon. Here's the $2 you left on the dresser. We don't want it, because we loved to have you." It was signed: "Love from Aunt Bessie and the Randalls." And then: "P. S. Here are some sandwiches and peaches to save you buying supper."

...Now, when I look at a map of North America, it is my fancy that another set of pictures brings it to life. Every one of scores of places glows, for me, with the face of some kindly person who gave me a hand or a laugh or helped on my journey.

The Friendship

In this charming story a little boy has fallen at school and injured his knees. The neighborhood policeman helps him home and teaches him that friendship is a noble thing.

The sergeant at once took third place in omniscience behind God and his father, and it occurred to Robert that perhaps he should put him first. The only flaw in everything was that his

protector had been unimpressed by his not crying when his knees did hurt so intensely. They reached the gate of his house. His mother stood anxiously on the front porch, since the accident had delayed him. He waved to her and she waved back.

The policeman said, "You might say to your mother that I suggest hot water first, and then an antiseptic and bandages." He cleared his throat. "You are a very brave young man. Many boys would have cried. I usually pass your school during the noon recess, and when we meet again, I hope we may walk together."

"Oh, I hope so too." He recalled his manners. "Thank you, sir," he said.

"And you are polite too. I'm sure we shall be friends."

He tipped his cap to the lady coming down to the path and strolled impressively away.

Robert cried out, "Mother, I fell down and I couldn't breathe, and see my knees, all bleeding, and a policeman picked me up and came home with me."

...He was unable to avoid boasting at school, just a little, for Sergeant Masters was waiting for him almost every noon.

The tough boys sneered, "Who wants a cop for

a friend? Yah. Bet your mamma pays him to take baby home. Yah. 'Fraid we'll beat you up. We don't beat up babies. Bet she pays him a dollar a week."

The idea had its unspeakable possibilities. His mother was often unduly solicitous. He did not dare approach her on the subject, but he did sound out the sergeant.

"Do you know my mother?" he asked one day.

"I don't have that pleasure. But...I am acquainted with your father."

Perhaps his father had hired the policeman. Perhaps his father had enemies and was threatened with the kidnaping of his son. This thought was exciting and acceptable, but it invalidated the friendship. He pondered over his next question. He felt very sly and clever as he asked it.

"A good policeman wouldn't take money for walking home with anybody, would he?"

The sergeant stopped and stared down at him. "Somebody has been putting ideas in your head. No, Robert, a good policeman doesn't take money for anything." He laid a huge, gentle hand on the little boy's shoulder. "I am your friend. Always remember that friendship is a noble thing."

Madami: My Eight Years of Adventure With the Congo Pigmies

When artist Anne Putnam married and left New York for Africa, the world's smallest people, the Pigmies, became her close neighbors. With her husband, who ran a medical clinic deep in the Belgian Congo, "Madami" Putnam became the little people's trusted friend.

Until I was married, painting had been my whole life. I knew that no woman had ever used pigmies as subjects, and I was eager to paint them in their natural surroundings.

When I arrived most of the men were off hunting, but a little fellow with a pointed beard and a potbelly seemed to be in charge. His name was Herafu. After greetings were over, he sat down coolly, and for an hour we carried on a not very friendly conversation through an interpreter.

Then I began to see the light. Obviously Herafu had stayed home because the pigmies thought I was coming to see if they were holding out on meat.

"Herafu," I said, "I came here to paint for a few

days. If there is meat, I will buy some. But if the catch is small, I will ask for none."

That did it. The atmosphere in the camp cleared immediately. In an instant dozens of little people were helping Pat's boys build a house for me, singing as they scuttled around. I felt like Snow White and the dwarfs.

Later I started sketching, working first with the women since they seemed more bashful, and I feared that any minute they would all take off for the forest. Herafu sulked by his fire for a while, then walked over. "I might as well go hunting," he said. "Perhaps I'll go to Mambasa for a few days."

I unrolled the largest piece of canvas I had. "Don't go," I said through the interpreter. "I'm saving this big one for you."

Herafu almost danced with joy. He strutted around like Soglow's Little King, posing and preening like a rooster in a flock of hens.

For a week I stayed close to the village, painting and loafing. It was like a small corner of paradise. The pigmies hunted, worked or danced as the fancy struck them; and all the time I felt as if I were living in an elfin dreamland.

The Wrong Turn

C. C. Marvill tells how motorists can find an un-expected — but welcome — friend in Switzerland; they have only to make a wrong turn.

We live in Lugano (Switzerland) on the main highway to the St. Gotthard Pass. Here the road divides deceptively, a new broad street leading to a remote mountainous region, while the narrow one is the main road. Many a motorist takes the wrong turn.

For some time now a white-haired man on crutches — very feeble and very old — has been standing at the crossroads and if a driver swerves toward the wrong road he signals "halt" with his crutch, then gives a friendly explanation. He speaks four languages, for we are all polyglots in Switzerland, and an unending line of cars keeps him busy.

"I am good for something after all," he told me the other day with a radiant smile. "And I have even made some friends." Proudly he showed me postcards from Michigan, Sweden, Brazil.

So he stands there, in sunshine and rain, the helpless man with the helping hand.

Reconciliation

In this heartwarming story, Pierre van Paasen tells of two priests who, because of their birth-places, find themselves on opposite sides of war. They fight their own battle — a battle of the heart — and they both win.

I dropped into the old Union Depot (in Toronto), which was part of my beat, and sat down among the crowds in the waiting room. Presently two priests entered and took a seat beside me. They spoke in French. This was nothing unusual in Canada, of course, but I soon noticed that theirs was not the quaint, almost medieval speech of Quebec. We entered into conversation when one of the clerics asked me in broken English how much time they had for the Montreal train. I told them the hour, and I added: "But you are from France, *mon Pere,* and not from Montreal!"

"*Ah, oui, oui, c'est bien vrai,*" came the answer. "But I have not seen France for twenty-two years."

"Twenty-two years! *Mon Dieu,* that is a long time. You will find the country greatly changed.

34

The whole north is devastated, right down to St.-Quentin and Arras."

"Yes, I know," sighed the priest, "but I learned all this but three months ago."

"Three months ago? You heard about the war but three months ago? How is that possible?" I asked. "The war has been over for three years!"

"We learned of the war three months ago, and not that it had finished, but that it had just started," the priest said. "You see," he went on, "we are missionaries, this father and I." He pointed to his companion. "We have been stationed in the interior of Borneo for twenty-two years. Three months ago, a Dutch trading expedition came to our station in the uplands from points still farther inland. From its members we learned that a war had broken out in Europe. Belgium had been invaded, they told us, Louvain destroyed, Rheims bombarded, Paris threatened. What we heard was incredible, ghastly: the massacre of civilians at Namur, the deportation of thousands of Belgians to Germany. To say that we were thunderstruck would be using a mild expression. *Nous fûmes annihilés.* The thought of that war crushed us, each in his own way, for I am a Frenchman, but my colleague here," he pointed again to the other priest, "this father is a German. We were in a most painful situation. For long years we had worked together as brothers, with never a cross word or disagreement ... then suddenly that news....

"For two weeks we could not bear the sight of each other. We avoided each other, each going his own way. It was dreadful. Yes, life was ebbing out of me, with sorrow and indignation. Then one day, as we met on the porch of our little church, both of us stretching out our hands to ring the bell for the Angelus, we burst into tears and wept on each other's shoulders."

A Thousand and One Lives

When his bus leaves without him in Switzerland, author A. J. Cronin makes some interesting new friends, and an unexpected event becomes a pleasurable experience.

Last summer I went on a conducted tour of Switzerland. One morning, in Bern, I was detained; no one noticed my absence and the bus left without me. I felt annoyed, but as my party would be returning on the following day I decided to make the best of my enforced stay. I visited the old town clock which produces a procession of antique figures at the striking of the hour, and then walked out to the famous bear pit. Here I asked a bystander where I could get lunch. The Swiss, seeing that I was a stranger, replied: "I am just going home to lunch. Would you like to join me?"

I hesitated at this unlooked for invitation, but accepted. I was introduced to the man's wife and two young children, and was soon made to feel at home. The Swiss was a watchmaker, and after lunch showed me around his small factory, explaining how the watches were assembled and giving me a chance to meet some of the workmen. When we parted it was on cordial terms and with the promise to keep in touch with each other in the future. Next day I rejoined the escorted tour, far from sorry at an occurrence which had not only gained me a firm friend but had vividly brought home to me an attitude of mind which cramps the lives of many people.

Some of us travel through life on a conducted tour, making friends only with the people inside the bus, keeping to the main roads and well-recognized centers. Then we realize too late that our lives are narrow, and complain that we are not fully living — forgetful of the fact that the remedy lies in our own hands. If we are willing to go off the beaten track, to make friends and acquaintances with people of diverse callings, we shall find our lives immeasurably enriched. In the words of the Arab proverb, "Let a man make varied friends and he will lead a thousand and one lives."

The Good Samaritan Taxi

On a cold, snowy morning, an old man demonstrates for F.A. Dann his own formula for friendship — giving of himself.

My wife and I were standing shivering in a blizzard at an isolated suburban bus stop in Calgary on a bitterly cold Sunday morning. Car after car passed us. Then a battered old coupe stopped, the door opened and a cracked voice shouted, "Come on, get in!"

We gladly complied and, although the upholstery was ancient and torn, it was warm and snug inside. The elderly driver asked where we were bound. Upon being told we were on our way to church, he chuckled and said, "Thought so. This is a taxi, you know."

Noticing our surprise, he explained. "Yep — the Good Samaritan Taxi. Been operating for

16 years and have never charged a cent...." He drove us to the church — two miles away.

Later, I learned that our driver was over 70, and that every Sunday for 16 years, in sun, rain or snow, he had driven his car to hospitals in the suburbs to take home nurses and interns coming off duty, and then had patrolled isolated bus stops and picked up stranded people. I also learned that he had no pension and that he worked for his living every day except Sunday.

Love Your Enemies —
It'll Drive 'Em Crazy

J. P. McEvoy writes here of the proverbial "turning of the other cheek."

Well, maybe it won't drive 'em crazy, but it'll certainly discombobulate 'em. Anyway, you can waste a lot of energy being nasty to enemies....

There are all kinds of enemies, and one of the arts of living is to learn to tell them apart — so you can either plow around them like a farmer plows around a stump, or get rid of them by making friends of them....

Let me tell you about one of them. She was the dark-eyed daughter of our village barber: a small, stormy, economy-size Gina Lollobrigida seen through the wrong end of a telescope. Years ago, I brought my two little girls up from Cuba in the late spring and put them in public school down the road. They talked a very peculiar language neither English nor Spanish — and their first and second grade colleagues gave them a hard time, naturally. Especially "Lolla" who was older and the ringleader Terror of the Tiny Tots.

Pat and Peggy came home crying almost every day, so I decided to cheer them up. "Let's have a party," I said. Pat's and Peggy's tears dried magically. Right away they got creative: "Ice cream! Cake, big red balloons!" "And friends?" I said. The tears started again. "We haven't got any friends," Pat blubbered. Peggy wailed. "Nothing but enemies."

Then I had one of my rare inspirations. "Let's have an enemy party. Let's invite all your enemies — especially the worst ones — and we'll fill 'em up with ice cream and cake and give 'em big red balloons to take home."

…Now the angels who have the special job of watching over children's parties must have been pleased to see that the "Enemy Party" was a mad, merry success, and the best time was had

by the biggest enemy, little "Lolla," who rolled on the floor and shrieked with delight....

One day "Lolla's" father dropped by to see me. "I came to thank you for asking my little girl to the party," he said. Then he added "...Nobody ever asked her to a party before. Why?"

A good question. Are the "Lollas" left out because they are enemies, or do they become enemies because they are left out? There are several schools of thought working on this but the Great Teacher settled it long ago. "Love your enemies, pray for them that persecute you, do good to them that hate you...."

And it'll drive them crazy, because it works!

A True Friend

Friendship is knowing how to comfort a friend. In this selection William Lyon Phelps shows just how important this knowledge can be.

What is friendship? Alas, I am able to give you an example. A number of years ago a very intimate friend of my college days, whom everyone had regarded as a perfect example of integrity, was accused in the newspapers of a crime. I could not believe it. I was so certain of his virtue that I wrote him a letter in which I said that I and all his friends were certain that he had not done anything wrong, that he had been slandered, and that he must not feel too bad about the attack, because as long as he had the inner certainty that he had done nothing wrong, he could remain calm and serene. I received a very affectionate letter in return, and then a few days later he committed suicide. Of course, I can't be certain whether I was in any way responsible for this tragedy; but what I am certain of is that I wrote him a very bad letter and that I was untrue in friendship.

Some years after this I was the subject of an attack because a press dispatch quoted me as having said something I really had not said. I received a letter from one of my former pupils. This is what he wrote to me:

"I do not believe that the report of your remarks is true. I do not see how you could have said that; but I want you to know that even if you did say it, my friendship and affection for you will always remain the same."

That is a good letter. That is friendship.

I'm Glad I'm a Little Guy

Carlos P. Romulo, Philippine diplomat and former president of the U.N. General Assembly, once explained his friendship theory in terms of physical height.

At the opening session of the United Nations in San Francisco in 1945 I was invited to speak as head of the very junior Philippine delegation. I found I could barely see over the speaker's stand. When there was silence I solemnly uttered this eight-word sentence: "Let us make this floor the last battlefield."

There was silence, then applause. I laid aside my prepared speech and let my heart take over. Words welled from me. Later I read in the papers some of the things I had said: "Words and ideas are more powerful than guns in the defense of human dignity....The only impregnable line is that of human understanding!"

The same words from a tall man might have brought polite applause. But coming from a

little fellow from a little country ... still one year from attaining independent status — they had an unexpected effect. From that day on, the little Philippines were treated as a full-fledged nation at the assembly.

We little fellows have another advantage: we usually have a special gift for making friends. People feel protective toward us, find it easy to confide in us. And most of us learn early in life that friendliness is as great a force as physical prowess.

Waving Good-bye

A friend is someone who's there when you need him. Such a person is revealed in this anecdote about a friend who waves good-bye.

Rupert Brooke in his youthful days was about to sail from Liverpool to New York. When he got on the ship he saw that everybody except himself had someone on the dock to wave them good-bye when the ship sailed. All of a sudden he felt lonesome. He saw a ragged boy on the dock. He went ashore and said to the boy, "What's your name?" "William," said the boy. "Do you want to earn a sixpence?" "Yes." "Then wave to me when the ship sails." With a dirty handkerchief this boy waved enthusiastically to his unknown friend until the ship was out of sight.

The Process of Friendship

Bonaro W. Overstreet defines friendship as "the process by which we pick...those with whom we have some deep communality of interest."

I cannot define friendship. I doubt whether anyone can. I do know, however, beyond all question, that I have richly experienced it and that I am indebted to my friends for no small measure of my confidence in life. Foregoing, then, the temptation to define, I can only say that there has been this person whom I have counted as a friend...and this very different person... and this other, and this other. Whatever friendship is, it must be a human relationship broad enough to take account of all these.

What part does help-giving play in friendship? I cannot answer the question when it is phrased thus. I know, however, that I myself stand indebted to many persons whom I have called friends. I know that between friends mutual help is as natural as breathing, and that the debt of each to each cancels itself out in the course of events. Also, I know from experience that an act of generosity can initiate a long friendship.

Headed west from New York on a lecture trip one winter, my husband caught the flu, and we found ourselves stranded in Chicago. We had young relatives there, but they had illness in their own home. Before we knew what was happening, however, they had passed along the word to another young couple — friends of theirs — and before we could think of hospital arrangements, my husband was picked up, carried off to their apartment, and tucked into bed. Having no spare room, the young couple moved out, turned their place over to us, while a friend of theirs moved into yet another friend's guest-room in order to lend them her small apartment.

For ten days this arrangement continued. Each evening the young couple came home for dinner with me; brought the food and medicines we needed; shared with us the day's happenings — and then trundled out into the January night to their borrowed beds. And they did it with laughter, with a flair for hospitality — and for living. Not their kindness, but *the manner of it,* laid the foundation for a friendship that has continued through the years....

More than once I have had the astonishing experience of making a friend in a few minutes or a few hours — and of having the friendship survive, with complete sureness, years of subsequent separation. One night in a crowded room, for example, at least two decades ago, my eyes met those of another woman and the twinkle in hers told me that we were making a like appraisal of certain ponderous pronouncements that were occupying the air. Spontaneously we worked our way toward each other and then toward a corner where we could talk. I still count her among my close friends....

Friendship is the process by which we pick out of the crowds of people we come across those with whom we feel we have some deep communality of interest. Our friends keep us from being too lonely with the concerns, faiths, and activities we have chosen — and we keep them from being too lonely. By being our friends, they lend us confidence that the basic things upon which we have staked our lives are worthwhile — and we lend them confidence. A genuine friendship is a stamp of approval that one person puts upon another's way of handling life.

The people in whom I have believed to the point of calling them friends — these have been so rich a sampling of the human race that, somehow, I can feel sure there are many more like them awaiting discovery. The people who have believed in me to the point of calling me friend — these, above all, are the people I must not disappoint.

An Inner Nearness

You live a little in your friend, and he lives in you, writes Morton M. Hunt, whenever you share common interests...whenever you share inner secrets and feelings.

Man needs an *inner* nearness. The English scholar C.S. Lewis points out in *The Four Loves* that companionship grows into friendship only when there is a mutual unveiling of secrets and a discovery by two persons that they have tastes or feelings or beliefs in common which each had thought his private treasure — or burden. "The typical expression of opening friendship," writes Mr. Lewis, "would be something like, 'What? You too? I thought I was the only one.'"

Sagely the Greeks and then the Romans referred to a friend as "another I" — the alter ego, the second self. And from that second self we draw strength to live. When I have a friend and he has me, each of us possesses more than his own little life, for I live a little in him and he in me. Each of us is a bit less alone in the vastness of time, less afraid of the dark, the unknown. We are still children in the woods at night, but we are holding hands.

The Unexpected Ways of Happiness

The art of making friends comes from deliberate practice, writes O. A. Battista. And from seeking friendship in often obscure places, we may find happiness in unexpected ways.

"If you want to make a potential friend a real friend," my father always said, "let him do something for you." I have since found that this formula works like magic even in converting a professed enemy to my side.

At one time, for example, I had an unfriendly neighbor who undoubtedly had reasons of his own to believe we were even less friendly. He wouldn't trim a single blade of grass beyond the property line or shovel a flake of "my" snow in winter. I knew, however, that he was a boiler engineer. One day when our boiler sprang a leak, I called on him as though he were the only person in all the world who could help me.

He came almost too enthusiastically, stomped down our cellar stairs, walked to a valve, and turned the water off. My wife and I smiled in admiration as the spray which had been squirting out of a pin hole in the hot-water tank slumped to a mere drip.

"You'll need a new boiler," he said with the attitude of a physician announcing a successful diagnosis. "But until you can get a plumber, I'll plug this leak for you."

Letting that man do me a favor turned the trick. We became real friends and pleasant neighbors....

By deliberately practicing the art of making friends, you may find happiness in many unexpected ways. Perhaps this is because we are usually able to handle grief and reverses on our own, if and when we have to, but to get the full benefit of accomplishment and success we must share our joys with others. As one retired man told me, and he spoke for the majority of retired men and women with whom I have talked, "I would say the secret of true happiness lies in

finding more than a normal share of the kind of friends you cannot have too many of."

One day I saw a young newsboy trip and fall into a puddle of muddy water with his stack of newspapers. I shall never forget the look of misery on that youngster's face. A half dozen or so persons had gathered when I stepped forward. "Say, fellow, you're going to have to come good for these papers," I said. "Here's a quarter to help you out." As I walked on, I noticed the other adult onlookers flipping coins. A block later a lad of 12 was at my side panting some of the friendliest things in my ears I've ever heard in my life. What a quarter's worth that was for me!...

Sometimes, stranger-friends — people with whom you brush shoulders for a minute or an hour, perhaps never to see again — can help us to see certain virtues in our loved ones that we overlook or fail to appreciate because of their nearness to us....

Ex-Enemies

Tami, a Japanese, and Pinkie, an American soldier, prove that friendship can be found even in the midst of a war. In his story Norman Cousins relates how these two men are able to rise above their former "enemy" status.

Tami's voice was high pitched and wavery, but there was no mistaking the fact that he sang "Show Me the Way to Go Home" as though it were the only song in the world. Then he went on to tell the story of his meeting with Pinkie.

"This song I have just sung was taught to me by a very wonderful and great friend, Private Orville Pohman. I met him on Christmas Eve 1945 at about three in the morning. It was snowing outside. I was sleeping. Suddenly there was a great noise. Someone was pounding on the door. Quickly I realized what was happening. The Americans were coming to kill me — just like my officers had said they would if Japan lost the war. At first I wanted to hide, but I knew they would find me anyway and would think I was a coward. I went downstairs to open the door. I was so frightened I forgot to put any

55

clothes on over my underwear. When I opened the door there was an American soldier, the first I had ever seen close by. He was a giant who could crush me with his bare hands. I looked at him and didn't say anything. I was trembling with fear. He looked at me and didn't say anything.

"Then he smiled and I thought he was laughing because I looked so funny in my underwear. Then I guess he thought I was trembling from the cold, because he took off his overcoat and put it around me. He smiled again and said:

"'Anybody here speak English?'

"I said, 'Oh, yes, I speak English.'

"Then he said, 'Thank God. I'm lost. My jeep went dead about a mile from here and I'm trying to find my way back to my barracks.'

"...We talked for hours....I was the first Japanese he had met who spoke English, and he asked me many questions about the Japanese people and about the army....

"Then we began talking about other things — about sports and music. I always have liked baseball and after a little saki we were showing each other how to slide under the throw. Then we began to teach each other songs. One song he taught me that night he said he had been singing to himself after his jeep broke down. It was 'Show Me the Way to Go Home.'

"Mr. Pohman...and I became very good friends. He brought me clothes and had them shortened so that they would fit. He gave me food at a time when Japanese had very little to eat. He gave me American books to read, history books and books about the American people. We played ball together. He came to see me three or four times a week. And every evening before he left we would sing together 'Show Me the Way to Go Home.'"

Father Duffy

Alexander Woollcott writes of a priest in New York City whose heart was as big as the city he served, a friend to all who met him.

(New York) is too large for most of us. But not for Father Duffy. Not too large, I mean, for him to invest it with the homeliness of a neighborhood. When he walked down the street — any street — he was like a cure striding through his own village. Everyone knew him. I have walked beside him and thought I had never before seen so many *pleased* faces. The beaming cop would stop all traffic to make a path from curb to curb for Father Duffy. Both the proud-stomached banker who stopped to speak with him on the corner and the checkroom boy who took his hat at the restaurant would grin transcendently at the sight of him. He would call them both by their first names, and you could see how proud they were on that account. Father Duffy was of such dimensions that he made New York into a small town.

No wonder all the sidewalk space as far as one could see was needed for the overflow at his funeral....One woman...saw an unused bit of pavement and asked a huge policeman if she might not stand there. He told her the space was reserved. "But," she explained, as if offering credentials, "I was a personal friend of Father Duffy's." The policeman's answer was an epitaph. "That is true, Ma'am," he said, "of everyone here today."

The Romance of Things

In this touching story, writer I.A.R. Wylie shows that friends give each other many precious gifts, and that among them is the precious gift of warm and beautiful memories.

A winter's storm was raging outside, shaking the old house so that it creaked in every joint. I sat huddled by the fire. And then my eyes came to rest on the sunlit picture over the mantelpiece.

For years it had hung there, but it was a long time since I had really looked at it. Now in the firelight the picture seemed to come alive: the Cornish fishing village became a real village with warm-stoned houses, the sparkle of quiet waters in the sun, boats in the little port drowsing with furled sails. I even picked out the window of the fisherman's cottage where I had lodged that far-off, enchanted summer.

Again I was sitting on the springy turf at the cliff edge, the sea gulls whirling overhead and beside me a young artist, busy with his paints and canvas. We had much in common. Both of us had been very poor, and both had known, ever since we had known anything about our-

selves, that we had to become what we were —
he a painter, I a storyteller.

The son of a Cornish miner, he had won
scholarships, fought his way to the Paris *atliers,*
starved, despaired. But now he was beginning to
make good. With his painting he hoped to break
into real success so that he could marry the girl
he loved. As the summer days passed and his
vision emerged on canvas I began to feel that I
had a part in it.

Back in America, I had a letter from my friend.
The picture had been exhibited by the Royal
Academy and now he had a possible purchaser
for it. But he wanted to give me first chance. I
wrote back with a modest offer, which he gener-
ously accepted.

Now my friend has come alive again in this
picture which had been the triumphant expression of himself, conjuring up for me a perfect
summer's day and, above all, the youth and
dreams that we had shared together.

Set in Goudy light Old Style,
a delicately styled original alphabet drawn
by the American designer Frederic W. Goudy
for the Monotype in 1905.
Printed on Hallmark Eggshell Book paper.
Designed by
Claudia Becker and Robert Haas.